Fever on the Land

CLIMATE CHANGE

written and illustrated by Stephen Aitken

magic wagon

visit us at www.abdopublishing.com

Published by Magic Wagon, a division of the ABDO Group, 8000 West 78th Street, Edina, Minnesota 55439. Copyright © 2012 by Abdo Consulting Group, Inc. International copyrights reserved in all countries. All rights reserved. No part of this book may be reproduced in any form without written permission from the publisher.

Looking Glass Library™ is a trademark and logo of Magic Wagon.

Printed in the United States of America, North Mankato, Minnesota.
052011
092011
♻ This book contains at least 10% recycled materials.

Written and Illustrated by Stephen Aitken
Edited by Stephanie Hedlund and Rochelle Baltzer
Cover and interior layout and design by Abbey Fitzgerald

Library of Congress Cataloging-in-Publication Data

Aitken, Stephen, 1953-
  Fever on the land / written and illustrated by Stephen Aitken.
     p. cm.
  Includes index.
  ISBN 978-1-61641-673-7
  1. Habitat conservation--Juvenile literature. 2. Wildlife conservation--Juvenile literature. 3. Endangered ecosystems--Juvenile literature. 4. Global warming--Juvenile literature. I. Title.
  QH75.A413 2012
  639.9´2--dc22
                              2011001875

Contents

Spring Fever

Temperatures all over the world are rising due to climate change. Many plants and animals are changing the way they behave. Spring is coming sooner, with plants flowering earlier and birds laying eggs earlier every year.

HOT FACT: Spring in the United States now arrives ten days earlier than it did 20 years ago.

Many hibernating animals are waking up early. In the mountains of northern Spain some mother bears and their cubs no longer hibernate at all.

7

HOT FACT: Scientists think that climate change has affected the flight plans of 20 billion migratory birds.

Fever in the Wings

Every year some birds make long journeys called migrations. The timing and distance of these journeys are changing. Some birds no longer migrate at all. They find plenty of food for their chicks right at home.

Other birds are moving their homes to cooler areas. Birds that are usually seen only in the southern regions are now appearing in northern areas.

COOL IDEA: The Audubon Christmas Bird Count has recorded the changes in location and behavior of birds for over 100 years.

Alien Plant Invasion

Plants and insects are moving farther toward the poles to find cooler climates. These new plants are crowding out native plants. Warmer climates are helping these invaders.

Retreat from the Heat

Many animals are moving to cooler places and finding new homes. Studies show that they are moving several miles a year.

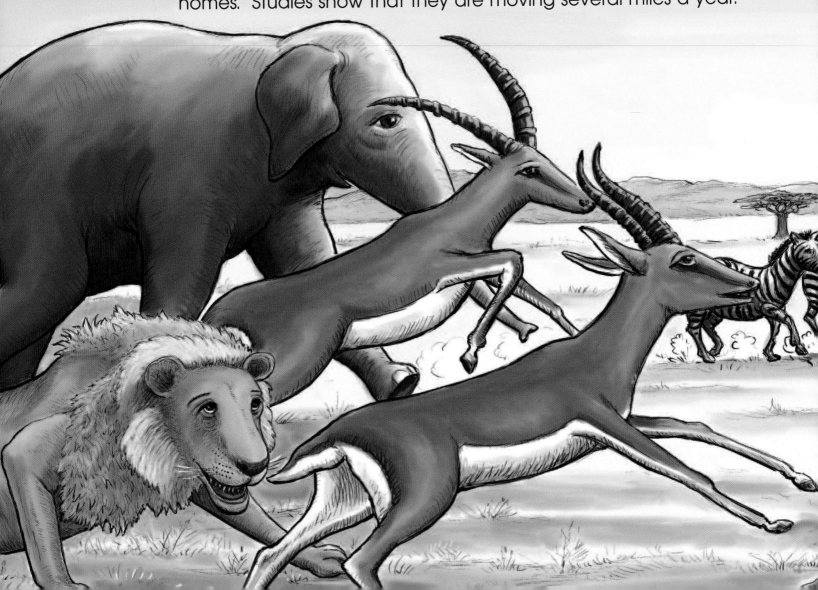

COOL IDEA: Scientists are now joining wildlife areas together. This lets animals move freely and safely to their new homes.

Animals and plants are also moving up mountainsides to find cooler places to live. Where will they go when the mountaintop gets too warm?

17

Fever in the Trees

Global warming has caused more forest fires. These fires now destroy twice as much area in North America as they did 50 years ago. The fires pollute the air with smoke and increase carbon dioxide (CO_2) in the atmosphere. They also destroy the homes of many animals and plants.

COOL IDEA: Smoke jumpers are specially trained firefighters. They parachute into the area near forest fires to control them.

19

Forests take in a lot of CO_2 from the atmosphere. This helps keep the climate from warming too fast. When we cut down and burn forests, climate change increases.

20

Forests are also threatened by an increase in insects. Higher temperatures are leading to more tree diseases.

HOT FACT: The pine beetle is a forest pest. It now destroys hundreds of millions of acres of pine forest in Canada every year.

Bug-o-meter

Bugs can tell us a lot about climate change. Many butterflies are appearing much farther north than ever before. But some southern butterflies are going extinct.

Butterflies and bees help move pollen from one flower to another. This is called pollination. Climate change means some pollinators may not be ready at the same time as the plants are flowering. The fever on the land is affecting all plants and animals.

26

HOT FACT: Hummingbirds love to drink nectar and pollinate flowers. Changes in their migration timing may cause them to miss the flowers that they pollinate.

Did You Know?

Young plants are called seedlings. Seedlings can be moved to cooler places when their environment gets too warm.

Studies on sea turtle nests in Brazil show that cold beaches produce more male baby turtles. Warm beaches produce more females.

The populations of harmful insects are increasing due to warmer temperatures. In 2007, bark beetles destroyed 5 million pine trees in Colorado.

Frogs are drying out all over the world due to climate change. They need water to breed and lay their eggs.

Large animals find it harder to stay cool. Studies show that over time animals adapt to warmer climates by becoming smaller.

Dr. Know Has Birds on the Brain

Birds can tell us a lot about changes in the environment. They take flight when danger arrives. They also move to new territories when the climate gets too warm. Scientists study the location of birds and their migrations to learn the effects of climate change. Here is an experiment you can do to learn about birds where you live.

What you need:
- A bird guide book
- Paper
- A pen
- A watch

What to do:
1. Study pictures of local birds so that you can identify them properly. Look at bird guide books from your local library or at an online guide like *The Great Backyard Bird Count* Web site: www.birdsource.org/gbbc/kids
2. Make a list with three separate days. Each day should have a different location—Day 1: At School, Day 2: At Home, and Day 3: At the Park. On each day's list, include the types of local birds you could see.
3. Go to Day 1's location with your list and a watch. Count birds for at least 15 minutes. Mark down how many birds you see of each type. Now, count the greatest number of birds of each type that you see together at any one time.
4. Repeat step 3 for each day on your list.

These lists are the kind of data scientists need to study climate change. You can help by going to the Web site in step 1 and joining The Great Backyard Bird Count in February every year. By entering your count, you can be a citizen scientist!

What Can You Do for the Land?

The change in Earth's temperature is almost totally due to human activities. People burning oil and gas for cars, trucks, and buses releases gases that trap heat on Earth. The power used to create electricity and other forms of energy adds to the problem. Here are a few things you can do to help keep the temperature from rising more!

Learn! Read more books about climate change. Then tell people about what you learned.

Be careful to not start a forest or grass fire. Don't play with matches and be sure to put out campfires.

Pollution can harm the water in streams, ponds, and puddles. Throw away or recycle waste properly to keep the land and water clean.

Help clean up your neighborhood! Join a group or ask your parents to help you start one to pick up trash and plant trees. This will make a clean home for the plants and animals near you!

Glossary

atmosphere - the layer of gas surrounding Earth.

carbon dioxide (CO_2) - a heavy, colorless gas that is formed when fuel containing the element carbon is burned.

extinct - no longer existing.

hibernate - to spend a period of time, such as the winter, in deep sleep.

invader - something that enters an area and takes it over.

nectar - a sweet liquid produced by some plants.

pollinator - an animal or an insect that carries or moves the pollen grains on or between flowering plants.

Web Sites

To learn more about climate change, visit ABDO Group online at **www.abdopublishing.com**. Web sites about climate change are featured on our Book Links page. These links are routinely monitored and updated to provide the most current information available.

Index